TODAY, I CHOOSE!

Starting the Day from a Position of Power

TODAY, I CHOOSE!

Starting the Day from a Position of Power

SHERI L. COOKS

W. L. C. PUBLISHING

2019

Unless otherwise indicated, all Scripture quotations taken from THE AMPLIFIED BIBLE, Copyright © 1954, 1958, 1962, 1964, 1965, 1987 by The Lockman Foundation. All rights reserved. Used by permission. (www.Lockman.org). Scripture quotations marked KJV taken from The King James Version of the Bible.

First Printing: 2019

ISBN 978-0-9820535-2-2

W.L.C. Publishing
P.O. Box 5123
Jersey City, NJ 07305

www.SheriCooks.com

Ordering Information:

Special discounts are available on quantity purchases by corporations, associations, educators, and others. For details, contact the publisher at the above listed address.

U.S. trade bookstores and wholesalers: Please contact **W.L.C. Publishing**
Tel: **(877) 554-5551** or email **Sheri@SheriCooks.com**.

DEDICATION

To Father God, Jesus Christ, the Holy Spirit,
my loving husband, Terence, Sr., and
our sons, Terence, Jr. and Malachi.

Thank you for being my inspiration and
the wind beneath my wings.

Thank you for empowering me to
start my day from a position of power...

Today, I Choose to love you...my best decision of the day!

ACKNOWLEDGEMENTS

I am grateful to my siblings and their families, my sister Sunya E. (Simeon) Okwuego and my brother Shawn R. (Laura) Williams for living the power of choice every day.

I am extremely grateful to my parents Roy and Thelma Williams who taught us that we have the power to choose, for explaining to us about the consequences of our choices, the importance of taking personal responsibility for our choices, and how to ensure that we are making righteous choices in our daily lives.

I am appreciative for the Pearls of Wisdom and Confidently Blessed Women Network for continuing to pray for me daily.

I am grateful to Renewing In Christ Ministries Church for the opportunity to serve you.

I am blessed for the continued love and support of my Mount Sinai Missionary Baptist Church and Mount Hermon Baptist Church families.

It is the love of this village that provides me with the inspiration to go after my dreams. To each and every one of you I say THANK YOU with all my heart.

CONTENTS

PREFACE

Blessings Beloved!

What an amazing opportunity God has given each and every one of us, the opportunity to make choices that will eventually shape our lives.

Do you know that you have the ability to create the life you want or better yet, you can choose to accept the good life that God has already designed for you? Ephesians 2:10 reads, *For we are God's [own] handiwork (His workmanship), recreated in Christ Jesus, [born anew] that we may do those good works which God predestined (planned beforehand) for us [taking paths which He prepared ahead of time], that we should walk in them [living the good life which He prearranged and made ready for us to live].*

Our Heavenly Father is extremely intentional about our lives. There is not a person on this planet that is an accident or mistake. We are divine decisions made by God Almighty the Creator of the Universe, Who gave us life, created us uniquely and necessarily different, and placed us in this time and space to accomplish a specific assignment that only we can accomplish.

Life is an exciting journey. The levels of joy and or pain we experience has everything to do with our choices.

This book is one of my choices. I wrote this book because I wanted to develop a tool to help you start your day from a position of power. A place where you choose to either accept or reject the situations and or circumstances that you face in life. Beloved, I know that you know this, but it is worth reiterating; you don't have to put up with or make do with anything. I had someone say to me one day, "you need to be grateful, it could be worst." The Spirit of the Lord rose up on the inside of me and reminded me of Whose I am and before I knew it, I said, "the devil is a liar! It could be better!" Change is possible! However, ALL change starts with a CHOICE! I care for you and I believe that you can make the choices that will change your life for the better.

INTRODUCTION

Life is all about choices. Our lives are a sum total of the choices we make every day. I created this book to be a tool to help you make an empowering choice every morning throughout the year.

Now morning doesn't necessarily speak to a physical time of day, but it speaks more so to a spiritual awakening – when you wake up to the truth that your life can be better. You have the authority to choose.

Did you know that when you make one empowering choice it can influence you to make another empowering choice? An empowering choice is a choice that comes from a place of authority – exercising your rights – that produces prosperity in every area of your life.

Empowering choices are sparked from knowing who you are, Whose you are, and what you are entitled to have and or experience. You have a right to live a life filled with love, joy, peace, fulfillment, health, abundance, wealth, and all the other perks that come from living life from a position of power given to you by Almighty God. The Blessing – an empowerment to prosper – is in your DNA according to Genesis 1:26-28 (*so God created man in His own image, in the image and likeness of God He created him; male and female He created them. And God blessed them...*).

This book is designed to help you start your day by making an empowering choice that will lead to you experiencing and living your best life. These empowering choices will positively impact your spiritual life, your personal and professional growth, your relationship with family, friends, and business partners, your physical body and mental health, your finances, and ultimately your outlook on life.

The first 90-Days is the "Starting the Day from a Position of Power Challenge." Each page presents empowering choices for the day, food for thought, and space to capture your decision for that day. You can start this journey on any day of the year. Simply schedule some time (20 minutes) to enter into your quite place, reflect on the choice, then make your declaration. I've provided a list of empowering choices for days 91-365 for those who desire to continue the life changing journey.

My prayer is that TODAY, you will choose to wake up and embrace the blessing – the empowerment to prosper in every area of your life. Let's start the journey!

TODAY, I CHOOSE: *Starting the Day from a Position of* POWER!

THE 90-DAY CHALLENGE – PHASE 1

Day 1
Today, I choose to start my day from a position of POWER!

This decision empowers my vision to see things not as they currently are, but how God designed them to be for me. Everything works out for my good and God's glory. Therefore, I commit to come to this place every day to reflect and take my position of POWER! What do you choose?

_____

_____

_____

_____

_____

_____

_____

_____

_____

_____

_____

_____

_____

_____

_____

_____

_____

_____

_____

_____

_____

_____

Day 2
Today, I choose life.

Life is good! It has both sunny days (good times) and rainy days (times of transitioning and preparation to receive the blessing). Both are necessary for growth and to experience my best life. Today, I choose to live. Today, I choose life. What do you choose?

_____
_____
_____
_____
_____
_____
_____
_____
_____
_____
_____
_____
_____
_____
_____
_____
_____
_____
_____
_____
_____
_____
_____

Day 3
Today, I choose freedom.

I refuse to live imprisoned by my past mistakes. I refused to be hindered by the negative perception of others and or self-defeating thoughts. I am living today in the liberty to experience the very best life has to offer. Today, I choose to live. Today, I choose to live in freedom. What do you choose?

_____

_____

_____

_____

_____

_____

_____

_____

_____

_____

_____

_____

_____

_____

_____

_____

_____

_____

_____

_____

_____

_____

_____

Day 4
Today, I choose peace.

I choose life without disturbance. All is well. What I am facing right now is transition – just a part of the process to experiencing my best life. So, I speak peace to every worry, anxiety, fear, doubt, and unbelief. I remind myself that ALL is well. I choose to live in the tranquil place of peace. (Read Philippians 4:4-8) What do you choose?

_____

_____

_____

_____

_____

_____

_____

_____

_____

_____

_____

_____

_____

_____

_____

_____

_____

_____

_____

_____

Day 5
Today, I choose joy.

I choose to take great pleasure in my transition process. In spite of what I see in the demolition stage, I take comfort and have peace knowing the final outcome; experiencing my best life. Happiness depends on what happens - my situation or circumstance. But joy comes from knowing something deeper that will bring a positive change to my situation or circumstance. ALL is well. I choose to live with joy. The joy of the Lord is my strength. (Read Nehemiah 8:10) What do you choose?

_____

_____

_____

_____

_____

_____

_____

_____

_____

_____

_____

_____

_____

_____

_____

_____

_____

_____

Day 6
Today, I choose love.

I choose to love God first. I choose to love Him with my whole heart. By doing this I can love me; knowing that I am created in God's image and after His likeness. When I choose to love myself, it empowers me to love others. God instructed us to love our neighbors as we love ourselves. If I don't love me, then I can't love others. Today, I choose to love. What do you choose?

_____
_____
_____
_____
_____
_____
_____
_____
_____
_____
_____
_____
_____
_____
_____
_____
_____
_____
_____
_____

Day 7
Today, I choose patience.

I will stay calm and allow patience to have her perfect work. I will persevere through the process of change and I choose to enjoy the journey. (Please read James 1:4) What do you choose?

_____

_____

_____

_____

_____

_____

_____

_____

_____

_____

_____

_____

_____

_____

_____

_____

_____

_____

_____

_____

_____

_____

_____

_____

Day 8
Today, I choose kindness.

Today, I will express benevolence. I will be good to others and I will be accepting of the generosity of others towards me. Kindness is the gift I choose to give to my community. What do you choose?

_____
_____
_____
_____
_____
_____
_____
_____
_____
_____
_____
_____
_____
_____
_____
_____
_____
_____
_____
_____
_____
_____
_____
_____

Day 9
Today, I choose to follow my heart.

I will flow in the stream of enthusiasm. I will live today with passion as I pursue my goals and live my best life. What do you choose?

_____

_____

_____

_____

_____

_____

_____

_____

_____

_____

_____

_____

_____

_____

_____

_____

_____

_____

_____

_____

_____

_____

_____

Day 10
Today, I choose to forgive.

I am fully aware that if I want to live, I must forgive. Therefore, I choose to forgive myself embracing the truth that my Heavenly Father is the author of time and opportunities. What He has for me is for me. Nothing is ever lost in Him. He is the Keeper and Restorer. I also choose to forgive others. I let go of resentment knowing that in this choice to forgive I not only choose to live, but to live free. There are many things that are alive, but spend their existence in a cage. Take a moment and think on that. (Please read Matthew 6:15) Today, I choose to forgive. What do you choose?

_____

_____

_____

_____

_____

_____

_____

_____

_____

_____

_____

_____

_____

_____

_____

_____

Day 11
Today, I choose to exercise faith.

I will put faith to work today. I will not be moved by what I see, hear, or how I feel. I will hold on to what I know, trust the process, and obtain the results promised if I don't give up, cave in, or quit. Today, I choose to exercise faith by putting total confidence in the integrity of God's Word and my covenant with Him. He cannot lie and He will not fail. (Read Hebrews 11) What do you choose?

_____

_____

_____

_____

_____

_____

_____

_____

_____

_____

_____

_____

_____

_____

_____

_____

_____

_____

_____

Day 12
Today, I choose courage.

Stop running scared! Our God commands that we be strong and very courageous. He is with us wherever we go. Today, I choose courage knowing that God has me covered! (Read Joshua 1:9.) What do you choose?

_____
_____
_____
_____
_____
_____
_____
_____
_____
_____
_____
_____
_____
_____
_____
_____
_____
_____
_____
_____
_____

Day 13
Today, I choose to live in the Anointing.

The Bible tells us that the anointing removes the burden and destroys the yoke. In Luke 4:18-19, Jesus reads what the prophet says about Him; that He is anointed to remove every adverse circumstance in our lives. And because I have asked Him to be my Savior and Lord, I choose to live free from burdens and yokes by trusting and obeying Him. What do you choose?

_____
_____
_____
_____
_____
_____
_____
_____
_____
_____
_____
_____
_____
_____
_____
_____
_____
_____
_____
_____
_____

Day 14
Today, I choose to trust.

You know, I came to discover that God is so much smarter than me. I know you're probably thinking, that's no divine revelation. Duh! Of course, He is!" But you know Beloved, there are a lot of people who have not come to that conclusion in their heart. This is simply information held up in their head. How do we know this? We know this because they continue to do things their own way even after "consulting" God. Trust is not a head condition; it's a heart condition! Today, I choose to trust God! (Read Proverbs 3:5-6.) What do you choose?

_____
_____
_____
_____
_____
_____
_____
_____
_____
_____
_____
_____
_____
_____
_____
_____
_____
_____
_____

Day 15

Today, I choose to believe that the impossible is possible for me.

Mark 9:17-27 tells of an account of a man who was dealing with what seemed to be an impossible situation concerning his son. He was frustrated and at the end of his list of possibilities. Jesus said "bring him to me." The man said to Jesus "if you can do anything have compassion on us and help us." Jesus, put it right back on him and said "If you can believe, all things are possible to him that believes." There is nothing that God's power cannot accomplish. Don't concede! Don't give up! Don't cave in! Don't quit! Give God your permission, your participation, and your cooperation by coming into agreement with His Word, operate your faith, obey and do what He instructs and commands. So today, I choose to believe that the impossible is possible for me. God is able!!! And He loves HIM some me! This is a good place to say, "Me too!" God is big enough to love, bless, and take care of all of us! I'm praying for you. What do you choose?

_____

_____

_____

_____

_____

_____

_____

_____

_____

_____

_____

_____

_____

_____

Day 16
Today, I choose to believe.

Today, I choose to believe that everything in my life is changing for the better. (Mark 9:23) What do you choose?

_____
_____
_____
_____
_____
_____
_____
_____
_____
_____
_____
_____
_____
_____
_____
_____
_____
_____
_____
_____
_____

Day 17
Today, I choose to dream.

Dreaming takes me away from my current reality to see the place where God desires me to be. My dreams make life worth living because they produce an expectation of experiencing my Heavenly Father's love daily. Today, I choose to dream knowing that my dreams are becoming my reality. (Read Genesis 15:1) What do you choose?

_____
_____
_____
_____
_____
_____
_____
_____
_____
_____
_____
_____
_____
_____
_____
_____
_____
_____
_____
_____
_____

Day 18
Today, I choose to listen to God's Spirit.

The Holy Spirit is God's Spirit. He knows the thoughts, plans, desires, Word, and Will of God. The Holy Spirit knows the truth. Listening to the Holy Spirit will always give me the advantage in every area of my life. In this world, there are many voices with a vast array of opinions. Today, I choose to listen to God's Spirit! Please read John 16:13. What do you choose?

_____
_____
_____
_____
_____
_____
_____
_____
_____
_____
_____
_____
_____
_____
_____
_____
_____
_____
_____
_____

Day 19
Today, I choose to receive direction.

The million-dollar question is…which way do I go? Believe me when I tell you that there are numerous people who believe that they have your answer. However, the only one who truly knows the way that we should take is our Heavenly Father and Creator. Please read Proverbs 19:21. Today, I choose to receive direction from God. What do you choose?

_____

_____

_____

_____

_____

_____

_____

_____

_____

_____

_____

_____

_____

_____

_____

_____

_____

_____

_____

_____

Day 20
Today, I choose health.

We have been given a wonderful gift from God Almighty called life. This gift in the natural can span the length of 120 years. Therefore, we should commit to live every day in a state of health – being sound in spirit, mind, body, and relationships – free from physical and mental disease and pain. Today, I choose to live the Word of God for it is life to those that find it, and health to all their flesh. Read Proverbs 4:20-22. What do you choose?

_____
_____
_____
_____
_____
_____
_____
_____
_____
_____
_____
_____
_____
_____
_____
_____
_____
_____
_____

Day 21
Today, I choose to take a walk.

Taking a walk is one of the healthiest forms of exercise from a natural and spiritual perspective as walking expresses forward movement. Today, I choose to walk intentionally in the natural for my health and in the spirit, I am committed to walking out my faith in the direction of my dreams. I am fully persuaded that I will gain momentum as I take our Heavenly Father at His Word. With Him, ALL things are possible. As a result, my health is better, I am achieving my goals, and realizing my dreams! (Read Matthew 19:26) What do you choose?

_____
_____
_____
_____
_____
_____
_____
_____
_____
_____
_____
_____
_____
_____
_____
_____
_____
_____

Day 22
Today, I choose to eat right.

Eating right speaks to more than just to what we put into our physical body, but it also speaks to what we are feeding our soul (our mind, will, emotions, intellect, and imagination.) Today, I choose to feed my physical body fresh fruits and vegetables and my soul healthy conversations, positive relationships, edifying reading materials, and uplifting television programs. What do you choose?

_____
_____
_____
_____
_____
_____
_____
_____
_____
_____
_____
_____
_____
_____
_____
_____
_____
_____
_____

Day 23
Today, I choose to take self-inventory.

1 Corinthians 11:31 reads, "For if we would judge ourselves, we should not be judged." Taking self-inventory is one of the greatest acts of love that we can show ourselves. It affords us the opportunities to take a look at how we show up in the world, appreciate the gifts that God has given us, how to use them for His glory impacting the world in a positive way, as well as, address the areas in which we need to improve. Today, I choose to lovingly take self-inventory. What do you choose?

_____
_____
_____
_____
_____
_____
_____
_____
_____
_____
_____
_____
_____
_____
_____
_____
_____
_____
_____
_____

Day 24
Today, I choose to exercise.

What a powerful declaration! Today, I choose to exercise. I choose to exercise my body to improve my physical health and I choose to exercise my "right to choose," which improves my mental and emotional health. (Read Deuteronomy 30:19-20) What do you choose?

_____
_____
_____
_____
_____
_____
_____
_____
_____
_____
_____
_____
_____
_____
_____
_____
_____
_____
_____
_____
_____

Day 25
Today, I choose beauty.

Today, I choose to see the beauty in those with whom I will interact. Today, I choose to express beauty in my environment by way of my actions, speech, and appearance. What do you choose?

_____
_____
_____
_____
_____
_____
_____
_____
_____
_____
_____
_____
_____
_____
_____
_____
_____
_____
_____
_____
_____
_____
_____

Day 26
Today, I choose to be considerate.

Today, I choose to be polite and kind even when there may seem to be justification for acting otherwise. I will be intentional in ensuring that I do not cause harm or inconvenience others today. I will show forth the love of God in all that I do, bringing Him glory as I may be the only expression of God's love that others will see today. What do you choose?

_____
_____
_____
_____
_____
_____
_____
_____
_____
_____
_____
_____
_____
_____
_____
_____
_____
_____
_____
_____

Day 27
Today, I choose to express a positive attitude.

I am so grateful that I belong to the Most High God. I am settled in my heart and mind that there is absolutely nothing that His power and love for me cannot see me through. Therefore, I choose to express a positive attitude with my behavior reflecting that which I believe. No need for a "poker face" today! (smile) What do you choose?

_____
_____
_____
_____
_____
_____
_____
_____
_____
_____
_____
_____
_____
_____
_____
_____
_____
_____
_____
_____
_____

Day 28
Today, I choose to be on time.

Showing up on time is one of the highest levels of respect. It is how we exemplify that we value ourselves and others. There is nothing more disrespectful and devaluing than someone who dishonors your time. Time is the only true "no refund" policy. Today, I choose to be an excellent steward of time and to honor myself and others by being on time. What do you choose?

_____

_____

_____

_____

_____

_____

_____

_____

_____

_____

_____

_____

_____

_____

_____

_____

_____

_____

Day 29
Today, I choose to experience the moment.

There is an account in the Bible of two sisters, Martha and Mary, who were hosting a gathering in their home which included a very important guest, Jesus. Martha was consumed with much serving, while Mary sat at the feet of Jesus as He taught. Martha asked Jesus to make Mary assist her. He expressed to Martha that she was worried about many things that were not important. Mary has chosen to experience the moment in which it will benefit her now, and in the days to come. Are you missing the benefit of being in the moment? (Read Luke 10:38-42.) What do you choose?

_____
_____
_____
_____
_____
_____
_____
_____
_____
_____
_____
_____
_____
_____
_____
_____
_____
_____

Day 30
Today, I choose strength.

We are stronger than we think. We can accomplish our assignments with the help of our God. Psalms 28:7-8 reads "The LORD is my strength and my shield; my heart trusted in Him, and I am helped: therefore, my heart greatly rejoices; and with my song will I praise Him. The LORD is their strength, and He is the saving strength of His anointed." Today, I choose to operate from God's strength. What do you choose?

_____

_____

_____

_____

_____

_____

_____

_____

_____

_____

_____

_____

_____

_____

_____

_____

_____

_____

_____

THE 90-DAY CHALLENGE – PHASE 2

Day 31
Today, I choose hope.

Beloved, our Heavenly Father has made us so many promises. He is extremely faithful and can be trusted. So today, when I choose hope – it is more than a feeling, but trust and expectation that God will do just what He promised. (Jeremiah 29:11) What do you choose?

_____
_____
_____
_____
_____
_____
_____
_____
_____
_____
_____
_____
_____
_____
_____
_____
_____
_____
_____
_____
_____
_____

Day 32
Today, I choose compassion.

Today, I choose to express compassion everywhere I go. I choose to be understanding and kind. I choose to leave matters better than I found them. I choose to exercise the power that God has given me to act like Jesus…do what He did, show compassion that changes lives! What do you choose?

Day 33
Today, I choose to get out of debt.

Today, I choose to end slavery in my life…I choose to get out of debt. I choose to get real as it relates to my relationships with people and money. I choose to evaluate my spending habits and identify the triggers. I commit to being truthful with me! Freedom is available, but I must first admit that I am a slave to debt, ask the Lord to help, then follow His financial plan. (Proverbs 22:7) What do you choose?

_____
_____
_____
_____
_____
_____
_____
_____
_____
_____
_____
_____
_____
_____
_____
_____
_____
_____
_____
_____

Sheri L. Cooks

Day 34
Today, I choose promotion.

Beloved, the funny thing about promotion is that people are promoted to the position in which they are exemplifying the level of work without the title or the pay. It is the technical person handling their assignments with the proficiency of a manager who is promoted to a manager. Promotion starts with a decision to be promoted. A change in mindset from the position that you currently occupy to the position you desire, and the corresponding action on the level of the position. Choosing promotion means that you choose to change – to "up your game" and work as unto the Lord, the One Who gives promotion. You can do it! (Read Psalm 75:7) What do you choose?

_____
_____
_____
_____
_____
_____
_____
_____
_____
_____
_____
_____
_____
_____
_____
_____
_____

Day 35
Today, I choose to start a business venture.

Beloved, in today's society you need multiple streams of income. We know that our financial security comes from our Heavenly Father, however, He provides by blessing the works of our hands. The more streams you have your hands working in, the more God can bless you. You determine how blessed you want to be based on your obedience to God and willingness to step out in faith. Consider turning that hobby into an official business! What do you choose?

_____
_____
_____
_____
_____
_____
_____
_____
_____
_____
_____
_____
_____
_____
_____
_____
_____
_____
_____
_____

Day 36
Today, I choose increase.

Psalms 115:14 says that "*The LORD shall increase you more and more, you and your children.*" To choose increase means to choose obedience to God. It's a powerful choice to make and one in which you will not regret! Every act of obedience to God brings provision. Please read Psalms 115 in its entirety. What do you choose?

_____
_____
_____
_____
_____
_____
_____
_____
_____
_____
_____
_____
_____
_____
_____
_____
_____
_____
_____
_____
_____

Day 37
Today, I choose to value my gifts.

Beloved, the Lord has blessed us with some amazing gifts that most are devaluing by not using them. Many are complaining about what they don't have, while not utilizing what they do have. The Word of the Lord says that our gifts will make room for us and bring us before great men. However, that won't happen if you keep your gifts hidden. Honor God today by valuing and using your gifts for His glory. (Read Proverbs 18:16) What do you choose?

_____
_____
_____
_____
_____
_____
_____
_____
_____
_____
_____
_____
_____
_____
_____
_____
_____
_____
_____
_____

Day 38
Today, I choose greatness.

Beloved, greatness is in our DNA. We were created in the image and likeness of our Heavenly Father who is the very definition of GREAT. Today, I choose to stay connected to Him. I yield myself to be used by Him for His glory. I choose to renew my mind so that I will not shrink back, but allow Him to use me to the fullest. (Read Psalm 147:5) What do you choose?

_____
_____
_____
_____
_____
_____
_____
_____
_____
_____
_____
_____
_____
_____
_____
_____
_____
_____
_____
_____

Day 39
Today, I choose to thrive.

Today, I choose to grow. Today, I choose to flourish. Today, I choose to take on new challenges and do those things I thought I could not do. I choose to stretch intentionally…Today, I choose to thrive. (Read Philippians 4:13) What do you choose?

_____
_____
_____
_____
_____
_____
_____
_____
_____
_____
_____
_____
_____
_____
_____
_____
_____
_____
_____
_____
_____

Day 40
Today, I choose to explore.

We are children of the Creator of the Universe, God Almighty. He has created a vast variety of amazing people, art expressed in nature, and breathtaking things. Today, I choose to travel outside of my comfort zone to inquire and learn about things in which I am unfamiliar. There is so much more than what I see! Today, I choose to explore. (Read Romans 12:1-3) What do you choose?

_____
_____
_____
_____
_____
_____
_____
_____
_____
_____
_____
_____
_____
_____
_____
_____
_____
_____
_____

Day 41
Today, I choose knowledge.

Although Today, I choose knowledge, I am mindful that all facts and information are not equal. So Today, I choose the knowledge that will benefit me the most – the revelation knowledge of God Almighty. (Please read Ephesians 1:15-23) What do you choose?

_____

_____

_____

_____

_____

_____

_____

_____

_____

_____

_____

_____

_____

_____

_____

_____

_____

_____

_____

_____

_____

Day 42
Today, I choose wisdom.

Wisdom incorporates knowledge, experience, and the ability to make sound judgement. But it is also the discipline to apply knowledge, the maturity to learn from past experiences (whether failure or success), and the courage to stand for and do what is right being assured of the final outcome. Today, I choose wisdom. (Read James 1:5-6) What do you choose?

_____

_____

_____

_____

_____

_____

_____

_____

_____

_____

_____

_____

_____

_____

_____

_____

_____

_____

_____

_____

_____

Day 43
Today, I choose understanding.

Proverbs 4:7 reads *"Wisdom is the principal thing; therefore, get wisdom: and with all thy getting get understanding."* Why? Because understanding – knowing the innerworkings of a thing – will help you to stand firm when wisdom is challenged. With understanding, you can strategically implement the process, stay the course, and reap the reward. What do you choose?

_____
_____
_____
_____
_____
_____
_____
_____
_____
_____
_____
_____
_____
_____
_____
_____
_____
_____
_____
_____

Day 44
Today, I choose favor.

Today, I choose favor, but not just any favor...Today, I choose the favor of God Almighty. I choose to believe and accept the truth that I am approved by Him, He is going to support me in the assignment He has given me, and that He is going to show me acts of loving kindness beyond what I deserve. God is going to bless the works of my hands. Thank You JESUS!!! You are the example of that favor in my life. Thank You for loving me! I love you!!! Today, I choose favor. What do you choose?

_____
_____
_____
_____
_____
_____
_____
_____
_____
_____
_____
_____
_____
_____
_____
_____
_____
_____

TODAY, I CHOOSE: *Starting the Day from a Position of* POWER!

Day 45
Today, I choose friendship.

John 15:12-14 is a powerful commitment of friendship. Jesus says this to His disciples *"This is my commandment, That ye love one another, as I have loved you. Greater love hath no man than this, that a man lay down his life for his friends. **Ye are my friends, if ye do whatsoever I command you.**"* Today, I choose to be friends with Jesus by obeying and following His commandments, then I can be a true friend to others. What do you choose?

_____
_____
_____
_____
_____
_____
_____
_____
_____
_____
_____
_____
_____
_____
_____
_____
_____
_____

Day 46
Today, I choose gratitude.

Gratitude is one of the most valuable power principles. It is the art of being thankful and expressing appreciation for an act of kindness that has been shown. Gratitude opens the door to the bonus of the blessing. Please read Luke 17:11-19. Today, I choose gratitude. What do you choose?

_____
_____
_____
_____
_____
_____
_____
_____
_____
_____
_____
_____
_____
_____
_____
_____
_____
_____
_____
_____

Day 47
Today, I choose inspiration.

Today, I choose to be inspired by the love of God. He created us in His image and after His likeness with the ability to create things that will be life changing and a blessing to our communities and ultimately impact the world in a positive way. Dearest Heavenly Father, please use me today to do or create something that will bless Your people and bring You Glory. Today, I choose to be inspired by You, in Jesus' Name, Amen. What do you choose?

Sheri L. Cooks

Day 48
Today, I choose to live my dream.

Today, I choose to live my God-given dream – the preview of the good
life that God has prepared for me through faith in Him. Listen Beloved,
don't be afraid to live your dream because it seems impossible.
Remember our God specializes in making the impossible possible!
Choose to live your God-given dream today. Please read Luke 1:37,
Ephesians 2:10, and Matthew 19:26. What do you choose?

_____
_____
_____
_____
_____
_____
_____
_____
_____
_____
_____
_____
_____
_____
_____
_____
_____
_____
_____
_____

Day 49
Today, I choose to imagine.

Today, I choose to imagine that everything that is misaligned in my life can be realigned and changed for the better. Beloved, we were created in the image of the Almighty. Therefore, our lives should reflect His glory – His manifested presence, power, and goodness in our lives every day. As I imagine, I begin to see solutions to problems and ways to be creative. Today, I choose to imagine. What do you choose?

_____
_____
_____
_____
_____
_____
_____
_____
_____
_____
_____
_____
_____
_____
_____
_____
_____
_____
_____
_____
_____
_____
_____

Day 50
Today, I choose vision.

Beloved, Ephesians 2:6-7 lets us know that we are seated in heavenly places with the Christ Jesus. This means that we are positioned to see things from a different point of view. We do not see things as the world sees them – limited and hopeless. But because of our faith in Jesus, we are positioned to see things like God sees them…and He always sees things from a place of victory. When we believe that victory is available; we won't quit until we see victory! Use your vision to walk in victory in every area of your life, TODAY! What do you choose?

_____

_____

_____

_____

_____

_____

_____

_____

_____

_____

_____

_____

_____

_____

_____

_____

_____

_____

Day 51
Today, I choose to be helpful.

Today, I choose to be the support and or resource needed to make things easier for someone to accomplish their goals, realize their dreams, and or to enjoy their life. Today, I choose to be helpful. What do you choose?

_____
_____
_____
_____
_____
_____
_____
_____
_____
_____
_____
_____
_____
_____
_____
_____
_____
_____
_____
_____
_____
_____
_____

Day 52
Today, I choose to give.

When I give, I put a supernatural law in motion…according to Luke 6:38 *"Give, and it shall be given unto you; good measure, pressed down, and shaken together, and running over, shall men give into your bosom. For with the same measure that ye mete withal it shall be measured to you again."* Today, I choose to give. What do you choose?

_____
_____
_____
_____
_____
_____
_____
_____
_____
_____
_____
_____
_____
_____
_____
_____
_____
_____
_____
_____
_____

Day 53
Today, I choose to share.

When I choose to share, what I am really saying is that I am in a very powerful position – I have everything that I need. How is that you ask? Because I am connected to the Most Powerful Source in the whole universe – Almighty God. He is my Source, therefore, I have more than enough of everything and He enables me to share. Remember, all you see is not all there is. (2 Corinthians 9:8-11) What do you choose?

_____
_____
_____
_____
_____
_____
_____
_____
_____
_____
_____
_____
_____
_____
_____
_____
_____
_____
_____

Day 54
Today, I choose to be generous.

Proverbs 11:24 tells us that *"There are those who [generously] scatter abroad, and yet increase more; there are those who withhold more than is fitting or what is justly due, but it results only in want."* Proof that we can't beat God in the area of giving. Today, I choose to stand ready to give and give even more than what would normally be required. I choose to be generous. What do you choose?

_____
_____
_____
_____
_____
_____
_____
_____
_____
_____
_____
_____
_____
_____
_____
_____
_____
_____
_____
_____

Day 55
Today, I choose family.

Today, I choose to embrace, enjoy, and nurture my family. Family is one of the best gifts that God has given us. It is in this very unique relationship that we discover our gifts, we are challenged to grow, and we experience genuine love. Regardless of what was or is lacking in the family dynamic, there is always someone there trying to fill in the gap, make up for the deficit, and encourage you to thrive. Are you that "someone" in the family? Today, I choose family. What do you choose?

_____

_____

_____

_____

_____

_____

_____

_____

_____

_____

_____

_____

_____

_____

_____

_____

_____

_____

Sheri L. Cooks

Day 56
Today, I choose to mend broken friendships.

Beloved, life is too short to live in a world with broken friendships. Often times, when we look at the reason why the friendship failed, we will see that it was over something that doesn't even matter now. Or we will see that time has allowed us to mature. It's time to reach out and get the relationship right. Today, choose not to waste any more time. God has so much more for you. Today, I choose to mend the broken friendships and be blessed! (Read 2 Corinthians 5:18-21) What do you choose?

_____

_____

_____

_____

_____

_____

_____

_____

_____

_____

_____

_____

_____

_____

_____

_____

Day 57
Today, I choose to make that important phone call.

Beloved, pick up the phone today and make that important call. Don't let fear stop you from communicating the things needed to move forward with your dream, vision, and goals. The positive response you seek could very well be on the other end of the phone. What do you choose?

_____

_____
_____
_____
_____
_____
_____
_____
_____
_____
_____
_____
_____
_____
_____
_____
_____
_____
_____
_____
_____
_____

Day 58
Today, I choose to take a leap of faith.

Beloved, taking a leap of faith is not a blind or irrational action. Actually, taking a leap of faith is the most calculated thing a believer in Jesus Christ can do. It means that you know Who He is, you have confidence in His ability, and in His love for you that causes Him to use His authority and power on your behalf. It moves Him to ensure that everything turns out well for you. Today, do your due diligence, then choose to take a leap of faith to achieve your goals and see your dreams become reality. (Read Hebrews 11:6) What do you choose?

_____
_____
_____
_____
_____
_____
_____
_____
_____
_____
_____
_____
_____
_____
_____
_____
_____
_____

Day 59
Today, I choose to enroll.

Beloved, today is the day to get off the fence and enroll in that class, join that network of positive people, or sign up to become a volunteer – share your gifts...whatever it is that you've been contemplating make the decision to enroll today. What do you choose?

_____
_____
_____
_____
_____
_____
_____
_____
_____
_____
_____
_____
_____
_____
_____
_____
_____
_____
_____
_____
_____
_____

Day 60
Today, I choose to be present.

Beloved, there is a significant difference between being "here" and being "present." Being here just simply means that I am physically in a place, but being present means that I am physically in a place, actively engaged, and ready to move in my calling and share my gifts. Today, I choose to be more than just "here." I choose to be "present!" What do you choose?

THE 90-DAY CHALLENGE – PHASE 3

Day 61
Today, I choose to be care-free.

Beloved, Philippians 4:6-7 says *"Be anxious for nothing, but in everything by prayer and supplication, with thanksgiving, let your requests be made known to God; and the peace of God, which surpasses all understanding, will guard your hearts and minds through Christ Jesus."* Today, I choose to be care-free. What do you choose?

_____
_____
_____
_____
_____
_____
_____
_____
_____
_____
_____
_____
_____
_____
_____
_____
_____
_____
_____
_____

Day 62
Today, I choose to engage.

Today, I choose to habitually participate in the actions that will lead to my dreams becoming my reality. My dreams are well worth the investment. Faith without works is dead. Today, I choose to engage. (Read James 2:17) What do you choose?

_____
_____
_____
_____
_____
_____
_____
_____
_____
_____
_____
_____
_____
_____
_____
_____
_____
_____
_____
_____
_____
_____

Day 63
Today, I choose to choose.

Today, I take back my power by valuing by ability and right to choose. No longer will I allow others to choose for me as if: I am incapable of doing so, I don't know what's best for me, and or I am not in tune with the dream God has put in my heart. Today, I choose to choose. I am assured that I will make the right decisions through the assistance of the Holy Spirit Who leads and guides me into all truth. He gives me perfect peace letting me know when my decisions are safe. Today, I choose to choose. (Read John 16:13) What do you choose?

Day 64
Today, I choose power.

Beloved, it has been said that knowledge is power. Well today, I choose to walk in the power of what I know about our Heavenly Father, His love for us, His ability to do the impossible, and His authority to command everything to come into divine alignment to work for our good and His glory. Today, I choose power! What do you choose?

_____

_____
_____
_____
_____
_____
_____
_____
_____
_____
_____
_____
_____
_____
_____
_____
_____
_____
_____
_____
_____

Day 65
Today, I choose the best.

Beloved, we are children of the Most High God – the King of Glory – the Lord God Almighty Who provides everything that we need through His riches in Glory through Christ Jesus, Who is God's very best. Therefore, we can exemplify the very best in everything we do; the best in our thinking, the best in our relationships, the best in our service to others, the best in our communications, the best in what we put in and what we put on our bodies, the best in where and how we live, the best in our transportation, and in every area of our lives. Today, I choose the best. What do you choose?

_____
_____
_____
_____
_____
_____
_____
_____
_____
_____
_____
_____
_____
_____
_____
_____
_____
_____

Day 66
Today, I choose positivity.

Beloved, I have heard it said that there is power in positive thinking. This statement has validity only if you know, are connected to, and have faith in the One Who has the power to fix and make everything turn out right. That person is Jesus! Please read Philippians 4:4-9. What do you choose?

_____

_____

_____

_____

_____

_____

_____

_____

_____

_____

_____

_____

_____

_____

_____

_____

_____

_____

_____

_____

Day 67
Today, I choose creativity.

Beloved, since we are created in the image of the ultimate Creator, let's choose to step out from the norm and use our imagination and gifts to bring something spectacular to existence. Today, let's choose to express our creativity. What do you choose?

_____

_____

_____

_____

_____

_____

_____

_____

_____

_____

_____

_____

_____

_____

_____

_____

_____

_____

_____

_____

_____

_____

_____

Day 68
Today, I choose positive influence.

Today, I choose to surround myself with those who exemplify positive influence. I also choose to be an atmosphere changer by showing up as a positive influence in every environment I find myself in today. What do you choose?

_____
_____
_____
_____
_____
_____
_____
_____
_____
_____
_____
_____
_____
_____
_____
_____
_____
_____
_____
_____
_____

Day 69
Today, I choose positive expression.

Beloved, there will be times when we may hear someone say that we need to "fix our face" because of the emotions expressed on them. However, the work that really needs to be done is not with our face, but the work needs to be done within our heart. When we "know" for sure that our God has the final say in every situation and circumstance...nothing, absolutely nothing can phase us! Today, I choose positive expression in every aspect of my communications because I'm reminded of what I KNOW – my GOD has ALL POWER! What do you choose?

_____
_____
_____
_____
_____
_____
_____
_____
_____
_____
_____
_____
_____
_____
_____
_____
_____
_____

Day 70
Today, I choose to dance.

Beloved, dance is a form of celebratory expression. Psalms 150:4 says *"Praise him with the timbrel and dance: praise him with stringed instruments and organs."* Today, as I reflect on the goodness of the Lord, I choose to dance like no one is watching. And if they are…oh well…God has been extremely good to me! What do you choose?

Day 71
Today, I choose to sing.

Today, I choose to sing unto the Lord a new song. I will not whine or complain. But I will sing unto the Lord of love and gratitude because He is worthy. And if the truth be told, if I lack anything it is only because I've failed to ask Father God in faith then command my situation to come into divine alignment with what God has promised. The truth is that our God is faithful! This is my new song; God is always faithful! Today, I choose to sing. What do you choose?

_____
_____
_____
_____
_____
_____
_____
_____
_____
_____
_____
_____
_____
_____
_____
_____
_____
_____
_____

Day 72
Today, I choose to laugh.

Beloved, Proverbs 17:22 says *"A merry heart is good medicine and a cheerful mind works healing, but a broken spirit dries up the bones."* Today, I choose to belly laugh. I choose to laugh hard and out loud. I refuse to let the unnecessary seriousness of any situation break my spirit and give place to "disease." Look at that word dis-ease, which is an abnormal condition. Again, today, I choose to laugh! What do you choose?

_____
_____
_____
_____
_____
_____
_____
_____
_____
_____
_____
_____
_____
_____
_____
_____
_____
_____
_____
_____
_____

Day 73
Today, I choose to be glad.

Beloved, Psalms 118:24 says *"This is the day which the Lord hath made; we will rejoice and be glad in it."* The Lord has gone before us to prepared some wonderful things for us to enjoy. I am looking forward to rejoicing today, whether it's because of something that the Lord does personally for me, or if it's because of a praise report shared of what He has done for someone else. My expectation is that *I am going to rejoice today! Today, I choose to be glad.* What do you choose?

_____

_____

_____

_____

_____

_____

_____

_____

_____

_____

_____

_____

_____

_____

_____

_____

_____

Sheri L. Cooks

Day 74
Today, I choose happiness.

Today, I choose to live in a state of well-being. Jeremiah 29:11 AMPC reads *"For I know the thoughts and plans that I have for you, says the Lord, thoughts and plans for welfare and peace and not for evil, to give you hope in your final outcome."* What a comfort it is to know that God knows the plan for my life. Today, I choose happiness – the perfect state of well-being. God's got me! What do you choose?

_____
_____
_____
_____
_____
_____
_____
_____
_____
_____
_____
_____
_____
_____
_____
_____
_____
_____
_____

Day 75
Today, I choose to be free.

Today, I choose be free. I choose the freedom that can only be found in Jesus Christ. Beloved, I choose to walk in the absolute confidence of knowing that if I continue in His Word then I will know the truth and the truth that I continue in will make me absolutely free! Please read John 8:31-32. Today, I choose to be free. What do you choose?

_____
_____
_____
_____
_____
_____
_____
_____
_____
_____
_____
_____
_____
_____
_____
_____
_____
_____
_____
_____
_____
_____

Day 76
Today, I choose to design.

Beloved, what is that creative thing that God has placed in your heart that you have yet to sit down and design – taking it from your heart, to your head, then to pen and paper? Do not let fear or the excuse of not having enough time stop you from seeing the wonderful things that God wants to bring into the earth through you. Today, I choose to design. What do you choose?

_____
_____
_____
_____
_____
_____
_____
_____
_____
_____
_____
_____
_____
_____
_____
_____
_____
_____
_____
_____
_____
_____

Day 77
Today, I choose to develop.

Beloved, now that you have written down the design, it's time to take it to the next level and develop what you have designed. Please don't get overwhelmed. The development process starts in prayer. You can do that…right? God will give you the answers, the knowledge, the understanding, and the wisdom that you need. Where He gives vision, He will ensure provision. Pray with expectation to hear from God. Amazing things are coming forth! Today, I choose to develop. (Read Mark 11:24) What do you choose?

_____
_____
_____
_____
_____
_____
_____
_____
_____
_____
_____
_____
_____
_____
_____
_____
_____
_____
_____
_____

Day 78
Today, I choose to build.

Beloved, during the development process of the design that God has given you, you will also need to build faith and character. This will help you not to get overwhelmed and start doing things in your own strength, which can open the door to compromise causing you to fail the integrity test administered by the world system. Today, I choose to build my character. What do you choose?

_____
_____
_____
_____
_____
_____
_____
_____
_____
_____
_____
_____
_____
_____
_____
_____
_____
_____
_____
_____

Day 79
Today, I choose to write.

Beloved, there is power in writing. Whenever we put our thoughts, dreams, and desires on paper they seem to come to life. Meaning that we have to do something with them; we just can't ignore them. Writing a letter to that loved one to express gratitude allows the sound of our voice to be remembered every time it's read. Writing the dream and desires of our heart challenges us to see how they can become a reality. Before we know it, the writings find their way into our prayer journal and when God gets involved…Watch out! He will give you the desire of your heart and your dream will become a reality. Today, I choose to write with BOLDNESS my BIG Dreams and aspirations. What do you choose?

Day 80
Today, I choose to grow.

Beloved, there is a natural expectation of growth. Anyone who tells you "don't ever change" – check that friendship – what benefit are they receiving by you staying the same. Anyone who tells you "you haven't changed a bit" – check yourself to see if your growth is being stunted. Anything that is not growing is dying…it may be a slow death, but it is dying just the same. Today, I choose to grow! What do you choose?

_____
_____
_____
_____
_____
_____
_____
_____
_____
_____
_____
_____
_____
_____
_____
_____
_____
_____
_____
_____

Day 81
Today, I choose instruction.

Beloved, instruction is a blessing. I don't know about you, but there are somethings that I don't want to learn the hard way. There are some children right now – and you may be one of them – who wished that the person who put together their bike would have followed the manufacturer's instructions. Had they done so, the bike would not have fallen apart and the child would not have gotten injured. I don't believe that the manufacturer sent ten "extra" screws with the bike. (Smile) Today, I choose to receive and follow instructions to avoid hardship and obtain the blessing! (Read Proverbs 8:33) What do you choose?

_____
_____
_____
_____
_____
_____
_____
_____
_____
_____
_____
_____
_____
_____
_____
_____
_____
_____

Day 82
Today, I choose to mentor.

Today, I choose to be a mentor sharing my experience with the next generation in hopes of helping someone to achieve their goals and realize their dreams. Today, I choose to share and mentor. What do you choose?

_____
_____
_____
_____
_____
_____
_____
_____
_____
_____
_____
_____
_____
_____
_____
_____
_____
_____
_____
_____
_____
_____
_____

Day 83

Today, I choose to say thank you.

Beloved, thank you is more than a polite expression, it is an acknowledgement of the emotional investment made by a person to show you love and concern. When you say thank you, it blesses the giver and opens the door for you to receive even more. People love to do for those who show appreciation. Today, I choose to say thank you. (Read Luke 17:11-19) What do you choose?

_____

_____

_____

_____

_____

_____

_____

_____

_____

_____

_____

_____

_____

_____

_____

_____

_____

_____

_____

_____

Day 84
Today, I choose to be intentional.

Today, I choose to be purposeful about my life. I choose to be deliberate about accomplishing my goals and seeing my dreams become a reality. No more sitting on the sideline. Today, I choose to be intentional! What do you choose?

_____
_____
_____
_____
_____
_____
_____
_____
_____
_____
_____
_____
_____
_____
_____
_____
_____
_____
_____

Day 85
Today, I choose to nurture.

Beloved, nothing grows "properly" without being nurtured. Things that are not nurtured often times grow out of control. Look at grass in a yard. You can immediately tell the difference between a yard that is well manicured and nurtured versus the yard that receives no care – weeds, crab grass, and dirt patches are normally their signature look. Likewise, when we fail to nurture our relationships and our health, we can allow undesirable things to settle in that can stunt our growth. Today, I choose to nurture my spirit, my soul, my mind, my health, my family, my relationships, my finances, my personal and professional development, and my community. What do you choose?

_____
_____
_____
_____
_____
_____
_____
_____
_____
_____
_____
_____
_____
_____
_____
_____

Day 86
Today, I choose to follow up.

Beloved, refuse to allow fear to make you procrastinate resulting in you not taking the step to follow up. Fear gets its strength by lurking in the area of the unknown. Remember what you know – there is nothing too hard for our God and **He Loves You**! Today, I choose to follow up! What do you choose?

_____
_____
_____
_____
_____
_____
_____
_____
_____
_____
_____
_____
_____
_____
_____
_____
_____
_____
_____
_____

Day 87
Today, I choose to follow through.

Beloved, now that you have followed up, it's time to follow through with the corresponding actions that are going to bring your desired results. If you've started a project, today is the day to follow through. You are more disciplined than you think you are. Remember, you can do all things through Christ Who strengthens you. Today, I choose to follow through! (Read Philippians 4:13) What do you choose?

_____
_____
_____
_____
_____
_____
_____
_____
_____
_____
_____
_____
_____
_____
_____
_____
_____
_____
_____
_____

Day 88
Today, I choose to get up.

Beloved, better is waiting on you. I want you to know, that no matter how long you've been in your current situation or the circumstance you are facing, Jesus has compassion for you today, make the choice…Today, I choose to get up! Read John 5:1-9. What do you choose?

_____
_____
_____
_____
_____
_____
_____
_____
_____
_____
_____
_____
_____
_____
_____
_____
_____
_____
_____
_____
_____
_____

Day 89
Today, I choose to start over.

Beloved, we have a loving Heavenly Father Who is the God of another chance. This additional chance not only refers to physical and or spiritual life, but it refers to everything that pertains unto life. He can give you the opportunity to start over in every aspect of your life, health, relationships, business, finances, education, etc....you name it. Today, I choose to start over! A fresh start awaits you. What do you choose?

_____

_____

_____

_____

_____

_____

_____

_____

_____

_____

_____

_____

_____

_____

_____

_____

_____

_____

Day 90
Today, I choose to "Go for it Again!"

Beloved, if you've read John 5 you may have noticed that the man tried several times to get up, to get healed, but every time he tried to get into the pool another person would step in before him. Beloved, there will be times when you will have to "Go for it Again" in your getting up process.

However, you must know this, in your "Going for it Again" the Lord is going to meet you and give you the choice to move past trying Him to trusting Him.

You see, Jesus only asked permission, "do you want to be healed?" Then He gave the instruction, "take up your bed and walk." Now the man had a choice, continue to explain his excuses and remain in the same condition or trust Jesus and be healed.

Listen Beloved, no matter how legitimate your explanation for why you are in your current condition may be, when God's Word says that there is a way for your situation to change for the better (healing, deliverance, provision, protection, peace, joy, love, improved self-esteem, freedom from oppression and depression, healthy relationships, etc.); your explanation has now become an unacceptable excuse! God loves you and He wants the very best for you! Today, I choose to "Go for it Again!" What is the "IT" that you choose to go for again? Choose to go after "IT" with EVERYTHING you've got! And remember, you've got a lot of help! You are never in this alone! God loves you!

_____
_____
_____
_____
_____
_____

TODAY, I CHOOSE: *Starting the Day from a Position of* POWER!

Sheri L. Cooks

CONGRATULATIONS & REFLECTION

Congratulations on staying the course and completing the 90-Day "Starting Your Day from a Position of Power Challenge!" I know you are feeling AMAZING and POWERFUL!!!

Let's check in and see how things have changed in your life for the better since you've embarked on this journey by reflecting on the past 90 days and filling in the blanks to complete each statement.

Before taking the 90-Day Challenge, I was (describe your state of being)

_____
_____
_____
_____

After the 90-Day Challenge, I am (describe results/lessons learned)

_____
_____
_____
_____

Now, I'm (describe your current state of being)

_____
_____
_____
_____

Please visit www.SheriCooks.com/TodayIChooseTestimony to share your life changing experience. I would love the opportunity to celebrate your success and your new powerful state of being.

Again, CONGRATULATIONS!!! Let's move forward!

Sheri L. Cooks

CONTINUING THE JOURNEY: DAYS 91-365

Well Beloved, here you are at day 91. There is nothing that can hold you back from becoming the person of power you were designed to be and there is absolutely nothing that can hinder you from achieving your goals and realizing your dreams. The key is to continue to make empowering choices and declarations every day.

On the pages that follow, I have provided some choices that you can reflect on and make your own declarations. Have fun with it, be BOLD and COURAGEOUS...exercise your FAITH. Know that if you put God first, walk in integrity, and purpose to be true to what you know is right you will never relinquish your position of power, but you will secure your divine destiny.

Get your journal and let's go to work. This is no longer a challenge, but your lifestyle!

Day 91
Today, I choose to move forward.

Day 92
Today, I choose to look ahead.

Day 93
Today, I choose to enjoy.

Day 94
Today, I choose to smile.

Day 95
Today, I choose to keep my promise.

Day 96
Today, I choose to believe the best.

Day 97
Today, I choose to expect great things.

Day 98
Today, I choose to see possibilities.

Day 99
Today, I choose to check on my neighbor.

Day 100
Today, I choose to collaborate.

Day 101
Today, I choose to spend quality time in pray.

Day 102
Today, I choose to read.

Day 103
Today, I choose to speak.

Day 104
Today, I choose to seize the opportunity.

Day 105
Today, I choose to advance.

Day 106
Today, I choose to provide opportunities to others.

Day 107
Today, I choose to celebrate.

Day 108
Today, I choose to take notice.

Day 109
Today, I choose to live my dream life.

Day 110
Today, I choose to set goals for my life.

Day 111
Today, I choose to achieve my goals.

Day 112
Today, I choose to take inventory of my finances.

Day 113
Today, I choose to address my credit issues.

Day 114
Today, I choose to save.

Day 115
Today, I choose to invest.

Day 116
Today, I choose to rejoice.

Day 117
Today, I choose to cook healthy foods.

Day 118
Today, I choose to accept the invitation.

Day 119
Today, I choose provision.

Day 120
Today, I choose protection.

Day 121
Today, I choose to be new.

Day 122
Today, I choose to lead.

Day 123
Today, I choose to teach.

Day 124
Today, I choose to be a role model.

Day 125
Today, I choose to pray for others.

Day 126
Today, I choose to arise from where I am and move forward.

Day 127
Today, I choose to go in the direction of my dreams.

Day 128
Today, I choose to live and not die.

Day 129
Today, I choose to be powerful.

Day 130
Today, I choose to be empowered.

Day 131
Today, I choose to empower others.

Day 132
Today, I choose to present the best me.

Day 133
Today, I choose to think.

Day 134
Today, I choose to step out of my comfort zone.

Day 135
Today, I choose to be resilient.

Day 136
Today, I choose to think outside the box.

Day 137
Today, I choose to be daring.

Day 138
Today, I choose to take a chance.

Day 139
Today, I choose to ask for what I want.

Day 140
Today, I choose to accept me.

Day 141
Today, I choose to declare that I am more than enough.

Day 142
Today, I choose to be the best me.

Day 143
Today, I choose to stir up the gifts that are within me.

Day 144
Today, I choose to go to another level.

Day 145
Today, I choose to upgrade my thinking.

Day 146
Today, I choose to go where I've never gone before.

Day 147
Today, I choose to get the information.

Day 148
Today, I choose to conquer fear.

Day 149
Today, I choose to accept God's love.

Day 150
Today, I choose to share good news.

Day 151
Today, I choose to dream again.

Day 152
Today, I choose to determine the meaning of my age.

Day 153
Today, I choose to live without limitations.

Day 154
Today, I choose to overcome obstacles.

Day 155
Today, I choose to breakthrough boundaries.

Day 156
Today, I choose to tear down walls.

Day 157
Today, I choose to determine my value.

Day 158
Today, I choose to embrace the good life.

Day 159
Today, I choose discipline.

Day 160
Today, I choose excellence.

Day 161
Today, I choose to take action.

Day 162
Today, I choose to create positive habits.

Day 163
Today, I choose success.

Day 164
Today, I choose courage.

Day 165
Today, I choose to create productive routines that lead me to success.

Day 166
Today, I choose to be brave.

Day 167
Today, I choose to be strong.

Day 168
Today, I choose to operate fearlessly.

Day 169
Today, I choose to cultivate inner strength.

Day 170
Today, I choose to remember that I am loved.

Day 171
Today, I choose to get involved in creating something special.

Day 172
Today, I choose to let go of the negative past.

Day 173
Today, I choose to learn from my mistakes and move forward.

Day 174
Today, I choose to be a blessing.

Day 175
Today, I choose to walk in confidence.

Day 176
Today, I choose to do the thing that fear has challenged me not to do.

Day 177
Today, I choose to take full advantage of the opportunity given to me.

Day 178
Today, I choose to embrace the gift of today.

Day 179
Today, I choose appreciation.

Day 180
Today, I choose to achieve.

Day 181
Today, I choose to experience something new.

Day 182
Today, I choose to expand my capacity to love.

Day 183
Today, I choose to act despite the presence of intimidating fear.

Day 184
Today, I choose to walk in the fullness of who I am.

Day 185
Today, I choose to walk in the authority of Whose I am.

Day 186
Today, I choose to take my rightful place.

Day 187
Today, I choose to sit at the table prepared for me.

Day 188
Today, I choose to do my best.

Day 189
Today, I choose to encourage others.

Day 190
Today, I choose consistency.

Day 191
Today, I choose to pay the price for success.

Day 192
Today, I choose dedication.

Day 193
Today, I choose to work smart.

Day 194
Today, I choose devotion to my dream.

Day 195
Today, I choose to express my full potential.

Day 196
Today, I choose integrity.

Day 197
Today, I choose to operate key success principles.

Day 198
Today, I choose to win.

Day 199
Today, I choose to never give up.

Day 200
Today, I choose to believe that the impossible is possible for me.

Day 201
Today, I choose to make up my mind.

Day 202
Today, I choose to schedule time to think.

Day 203
Today, I choose to live in the now.

Day 204
Today, I choose to operate my faith.

Day 205
Today, I choose to be optimistic about my future.

Day 206
Today, I choose to do more than I did yesterday.

Day 207
Today, I choose to go further than I did yesterday.

Day 208
Today, I choose to be me.

Day 209
Today, I choose to get clear on my values.

Day 210
Today, I choose authenticity.

Day 211
Today, I choose to stand up for what is right.

Day 212
Today, I choose to take another step.

Day 213
Today, I choose to embrace the process needed to achieve my goals.

Day 214
Today, I choose to master my emotions.

Day 215
Today, I choose to take care of my emotional health.

Day 216
Today, I choose to forgive myself.

Day 217
Today, I choose to forgive _____.

Day 218
Today, I choose honesty.

Day 219
Today, I choose to share the truth in love.

Day 220
Today, I choose to embrace my leadership capabilities.

Day 221
Today, I choose to learn something new.

Day 222
Today, I choose to refresh my skills.

Day 223
Today, I choose to take responsibility for _____.

Day 224
Today, I choose to embrace my greatness.

Day 225
Today, I choose to lead with my heart.

Day 226
Today, I choose to be the voice of peace.

Day 227
Today, I choose to run my own race.

Day 228
Today, I choose to march to the beat of my own drum.

Day 229
Today, I choose to be led by the Holy Spirit.

Day 230
Today, I choose to show mercy.

Day 231
Today, I choose to yield my will to God's will.

Day 232
Today, I choose to rewrite my story.

Day 233
Today, I choose to take back my power.

Day 234
Today, I choose to redefine me.

Day 235
Today, I choose to get off the sideline.

Day 236
Today, I choose to define my destiny.

Day 237
Today, I choose to actively participate in life.

Day 238
Today, I choose to go bravely into the future.

Day 239
Today, I choose to be loved.

Day 240
Today, I choose Jesus.

Day 241
Today, I choose to focus.

Day 242
Today, I choose purpose.

Day 243
Today, I choose not to be distracted.

Day 244
Today, I choose to live on purpose.

Day 245
Today, I choose passion.

Day 246
Today, I choose to follow my passion.

Day 247
Today, I choose to do better than I did yesterday.

Day 248
Today, I choose to do those things that are important to me.

Day 249
Today, I choose to connect with family and friends.

Day 250
Today, I choose to take time for me.

Day 251
Today, I choose time to rest my _____.

Day 252
Today, I choose to manage my time wisely.

Day 253
Today, I choose to mature in _____.

Day 254
Today, I choose to move away from petty things, conversations, and people.

Day 255
Today, I choose to share company with big thinkers.

Day 256
Today, I choose to surround myself with positive dreamers.

Day 257
Today, I choose to exercise childlike faith.

Day 258
Today, I choose to let my imagination soar.

Day 259
Today, I choose to give myself permission to _____.

Day 260
Today, I choose to take control of the narrative of my life.

Day 261
Today, I choose to increase my productivity.

Day 262
Today, I choose to live my moral compass.

Day 263
Today, I choose to laugh out loud.

Day 264
Today, I choose to let my light shine.

Day 265
Today, I choose to be unapologetically me.

Day 266
Today, I choose to live with a fresh new excitement.

Day 267
Today, I choose wealth.

Day 268
Today, I choose to cultivate a prosperous mindset.

Day 269
Today, I choose to honor God with my finances by supporting Life-changing Kingdom causes.

Day 270
Today, I choose to live a life of abundance.

Day 271
Today, I choose to be blessed by honoring God with my tithe.

Day 272
Today, I choose to be generous.

Day 273
Today, I choose to receive generosity.

Day 274
Today, I choose to use the gifts God has given me to be a blessing to society.

Day 275
Today, I choose to welcome peace into my home.

Day 276
Today, I choose to resolve conflicts quickly and lovingly.

Day 277
Today, I choose to be approachable and easy to talk to.

Day 278
Today, I choose to be affectionate.

Day 279
Today, I choose to avoid strife.

Day 280
Today, I choose to find a new way to have good, clean fun.

Day 281
Today, I choose to allow my inner child of optimism to play.

Day 282
Today, I choose to honor God in my decisions.

Day 283
Today, I choose to honor my family in my decisions.

Day 284
Today, I choose to take care of my mental health by reflecting on everything good.

Day 285
Today, I choose to get organized.

Day 286
Today, I choose to leave an inheritance for my loved ones.

Day 287
Today, I choose to create something useful for the next generation.

Day 288
Today, I choose to leave every space I've occupied better than I found it.

Day 289
Today, I choose to hold on to my faith.

Day 290
Today, I choose to continue until I win; I will not give up so easy.

Day 291
Today, I choose to think well of me; I am more than capable.

Day 292
Today, I choose to think well of others.

Day 293
Today, I choose to be led by the Holy Spirit.

Day 294
Today, I choose to expect that something amazingly wonderful is going to happen through me, with me, and for me.

Day 295
Today, I choose not to settle.

Day 296
Today, I choose to embrace my uniqueness.

Day 297
Today, I choose to be bold.

Day 298
Today, I choose to embrace the beauty of me.

Day 299
Today, I choose to embrace the beauty in others.

Day 300
Today, I choose to respect myself.

Day 301
Today, I choose to respect others.

Day 302
Today, I choose to flow with time.

Day 303
Today, I choose to walk in the fruits of the Spirit.

Day 304
Today, I choose to live life to the fullest.

Day 305
Today, I choose to express an ethical character.

Day 306
Today, I choose to walk in integrity.

Day 307
Today, I choose to exercise my faith.

Day 308
Today, I choose to take a new route.

Day 309
Today, I choose to show myself friendly.

Day 310
Today, I choose to pay someone a compliment.

Day 311
Today, I choose to lift someone's spirit.

Day 312
Today, I choose to take personal inventory.

Day 313
Today, I choose to express gratitude.

Day 314
Today, I choose to repent.

Day 315
Today, I choose to see the Kingdom.

Day 316
Today, I choose not to concede.

Day 317
Today, I choose to start that project.

Day 318
Today, I choose to say yes to my dreams.

Day 319
Today, I choose to get the information needed to dispel the myths that have been holding me back.

Day 320
Today, I choose to volunteer.

Day 321
Today, I choose to pray for others.

Day 322
Today, I choose to check in on my extended family.

Day 323
Today, I choose to plan my vacation.

Day 324
Today, I choose to support the dreams of another.

Day 325
Today, I choose to encourage a young entrepreneur.

Day 326
Today, I choose to connect with my neighbors.

Day 327
Today, I choose to reconnect with old friends.

Day 328
Today, I choose to be persistent in following my beliefs and going after my dreams.

Day 329
Today, I choose to give.

Day 330
Today, I choose to conquer fear.

Day 331
Today, I choose to lay the foundation for the next stage of my life.

Day 332
Today, I choose to set goals that align with my dreams.

Day 333
Today, I choose to embrace that I can no longer go unseen.

Day 334
Today, I choose to step out into the forefront.

Day 335
Today, I choose to let go of every negative stigma.

Day 336
Today, I choose to manage my thoughts.

Day 337
Today, I choose to think on things that are true and lovely.

Day 338
Today, I choose to promote life.

Day 339
Today, I choose to become the person of my dreams.

Day 340
Today, I choose to use my imagination and dream...dream BIG!

Day 341
Today, I choose to remember that life is a gift.

Day 342
Today, I choose to live life to the fullest.

Day 343
Today, I choose to remember that I am blessed.

Day 344
Today, I choose to simplify my life.

Day 345
Today, I choose progress.

Day 346
Today, I choose to be intentionally in motion.

Day 347
Today, I choose to study the Word of God.

Day 348
Today, I choose to donate.

Day 349
Today, I choose to keep company with love.

Day 350
Today, I choose to forgive again.

Day 351
Today, I choose to embrace my future; it's bright!

Day 352
Today, I choose to worship God.

Day 353
Today, I choose to remember that God is my Source.

Day 354
Today, I choose to acknowledge that God is with me; there is nothing to fear.

Day 355
Today, I choose to change my position; to level up in my knowledge of God.

Day 356
Today, I choose to re-evaluate what is really important.

Day 357
Today, I choose to make new exciting memories.

Day 358
Today, I choose to cherish my family and friends.

Day 359
Today, I choose to draw my strength from God.

Day 360
Today, I choose to be unstoppable.

Day 361
Today, I choose to receive God's thoughts and plans for me.

Day 362
Today, I choose to express elegance and or the exceptional.

Day 363
Today, I choose to express wisdom.

Day 364
Today, I choose to mine my business…There is great wealth in me.

Day 365
Today, I choose to embrace the blessing – the empowerment to prosper in every area of my life!

Sheri L. Cooks

TODAY, I CHOOSE: *Starting the Day from a Position of* POWER!

REMAINING IN POWER

Wow! Look at you; powerful one. I am godly proud of you. What an accomplishment; you've stuck with your decision to choose a different course for your life …a better life. Reflect and share…How does it feel?

_____
_____
_____
_____
_____
_____

Well, all I can say is…Welcome to your new life! This position of power is where you belong. And in order to continue to operate from this position of power you must decide in this new season…

Day 1
Today, I choose to continue on with God's leading.

For more information on products and services designed to help you achieve personal and professional growth, please visit www.SheriCooks.com.

Again, Congratulation and Be Blessed!

Sheri L. Cooks

ABOUT THE AUTHOR

Sheri L. Cooks, BSM, CCLC, is blessed to be a wife, mother, life and success coach, spiritual leader, speaker, retreat host, and the CEO of Sheri Cooks LLC a professional and personal development company designed to equip people with tools to promote creativity, increase productivity, and move into successful and transformative thinking that allows the opportunity to win in both business and life.

Coach Sheri is in service to uplift others through the Confidently Blessed Women Network (CBWN) where she has the pleasure of serving women who share in the CBWN philosophy in their endeavors to use their gifts and talents to be a blessing to their families, communities, and in their respective businesses and or industries. The network provides monthly group coaching sessions and accountability services for its members.

Sheri holds a Bachelors Science degree in Business Management from the University of Phoenix and a Christian Life Coaching Certification from Professional Coaching and Counseling Academy. Sheri's innate ability to evaluate and identify intricate details necessary to achieve goals has afforded her to create systems that enables her clients to manifest success in every area of their lives and business.

Sheri is enjoying a rich life of 26 years – and counting – of marriage to Mr. Terence R. Cooks, Sr. that has produced two wonderful sons (Terence, Jr. and Malachi).

Coach Sheri is passionate about helping her clients achieve their goals and live their best life – the life of their dreams. It has been said about Coach Sheri, if you want to have a pity party call a girlfriend, but if you are serious about achieving results…call Coach Sheri!

For more information about upcoming Transformational VIP Days, CBWN Retreats, products, coaching services, and how to book Sheri L. Cooks for your next event, visit www.SheriCooks.com, email Sheri@SheriCooks.com, or call (877) 554-5551.